Better Homes and Gardens®

Silly Snacks

Better Homes and Gardens® Books
Des Moines, Iowa

Better Homes and Gardens® Books
An imprint of Meredith® Books

Silly Snacks
Editor: Jennifer Dorland Darling
Contributing Editors: Carol Dahlstrom, Shelli McConnell, Marty Schiel, Mary Major Williams
Design and Illustration: Wayne Vincent & Associates
Copy Chief: Catherine Hamrick
Copy and Production Editor: Terri Fredrickson
Contributing Copy Editor: Jennifer Speer Ramundt
Contributing Proofreaders: Kathy Eastman, Gretchen Kaufmann, Susie Kling, Wini Moranville
Electronic Production Coordinator: Paula Forest
Editorial and Design Assistants: Judy Bailey, Treesa Landry, Karen Schirm
Test Kitchen Director: Sharon Stilwell
Test Kitchen Product Supervisor: Jill Hoefler
Photographer: Jim Krantz
Food Stylists: Dianna Nolin, Jennifer LaMontia
Production Director: Douglas M. Johnston
Production Manager: Pam Kvitne
Assistant Prepress Manager: Marjorie J. Schenkelberg

Meredith® Books
Editor in Chief: James D. Blume
Design Director: Matt Strelecki
Managing Editor: Gregory H. Kayko
Executive Food Editor: Lisa Holderness

Director, Sales & Marketing, Retail: Michael A. Peterson
Director, Sales & Marketing, Special Markets: Rita McMullen
Director, Sales & Marketing, Home & Garden Center Channel: Ray Wolf
Director, Operations: George A. Susral

Vice President, General Manager: Jamie L. Martin

Better Homes and Gardens® Magazine
Editor in Chief: Jean LemMon
Executive Food Editor: Nancy Byal

Meredith Publishing Group
President, Publishing Group: Christopher M. Little
Vice President, Consumer Marketing & Development: Hal Oringer

Meredith Corporation
Chairman and Chief Executive Officer: William T. Kerr

Chairman of the Executive Committee: E. T. Meredith III

All of us at Better Homes and Gardens® Books are dedicated to providing you with the information and ideas you need to create delicious foods. We welcome your comments and suggestions. Write to us at: Better Homes and Gardens® Books, Cookbook Editorial Department, 1716 Locust St., Des Moines, IA 50309-3023.

If you would like to order additional copies of any of our books, check with your local bookstore.

Our seal assures you that every recipe in **Silly Snacks** has been tested in the Better Homes and Gardens® Test Kitchen. This means that each recipe is practical and reliable, and meets our high standards of taste appeal. We guarantee your satisfaction with this book for as long as you own it.

CONTENTS

ARE YOU BUMMED about boring snacks? Hey, check this out—**SILLY SNACKS**, a cookbook just for you. No dull stuff allowed—just totally great munchies.

GRUB ON OLD WEST TRAIL MIX and crispy nachos. Sip a tall drink—for cool dudes only. Make magic in the kitchen with secret potions, concoctions, and snacks that disappear (with a little help from hungry friends). If you want to really get weird, try some moon rocks, shooting stars, and other outerspace nibbles. (The space shuttle crews never had it so good.)

YOU'LL FIND excellent food adventures on every page. And you don't have to be a super chef to make crazy snacks. You can do it. Just ask Mom or Dad if you need a little coaching.

SILLY SNACKS—they're awesome! Really.

Super Simple SNACKS

FROZEN YOGURT-STUFFED PEARS

Cut a pear lengthwise in half. Using a spoon or a melon baller, scoop out the core. Place each half in a small bowl. Using a small scoop or melon baller, scoop balls of cherry, strawberry, or vanilla frozen yogurt into the centers of the pear halves. Sprinkle with granola.

FROSTY FRUIT

Line a baking pan with plastic wrap. Cover it with a single layer of your favorite fresh fruits, such as seedless grapes, strawberry halves, and melon chunks. Cover with another piece of plastic wrap. Freeze the fruit for 2 to 3 hours or until frozen. Serve the frozen fruit plain or with fruit-flavored yogurt for dipping. If you like, place any remaining frozen fruit in a freezer bag and keep in the freezer for up to 3 days.

Super Simple SNACKS

EASY BANANA PUDDING

Slice half of a banana. Stir together a single-serving container of vanilla or chocolate pudding and the banana slices. Sprinkle with crumbled graham crackers, crisp cereal, or chopped candy-coated peanut butter pieces.

FRUIT 'N' YOGURT CONES

In an ice cream cone, layer cut-up mixed fresh fruit, such as kiwifruit, strawberries, raspberries, blueberries, pears, or peaches with vanilla yogurt.

CHEESE AND APPLE SAILBOATS

Cut a small apple into 4 wedges and remove the core. Cut 4 slices of your favorite cheese (or use presliced cheese). Trim cheese slices to make triangles resembling sails. Thread the cheese triangles on wooden toothpicks. Stick them into the apple wedges for sails.

Taco Circles

Spread a popped corn-flavored or white cheddar-flavored corn cake with salsa. Sprinkle with shredded reduced-fat cheese. Place on a microwave-safe plate. Microwave on high for 15 to 30 seconds or until the cheese just begins to melt. If you like, top with chopped tomato, sliced green onion, or chopped green sweet pepper.

SWEET 'N' SOUR VEGGIE ROLL-UP

Stir together about ½ cup thawed and drained loose-pack frozen vegetables (or leftover cooked rice), 1 tablespoon drained pineapple tidbits, and 1 tablespoon bottled sweet-and-sour sauce (or any flavor of salad dressing). Place a flour tortilla on a microwave-safe plate. Spoon the vegetable mixture onto one side of the tortilla and roll up the tortilla. Microwave on high for about 30 seconds or until warm.

STACKIN' SNACKS

Cut out shapes from thin slices of cheese and cooked ham using a small metal cookie cutter. Alternately stack 2 or 3 slices of the cheese and ham shapes on a cracker. If you like, spread a little honey mustard between each layer.

WAGON WHEEL BISCUITS

Say "westward ho!" to after school hunger.

UTENSILS

Wooden board or pastry cloth
Rolling pin
Baking sheet
Small triangle-shape cookie cutter or sharp knife
Small microwave-safe bowl or small saucepan
Waxed paper (if using microwave)
Small bowl or custard cup
Spoon
Pastry brush
Hot pads
Pancake turner
Wire cooling rack

INGREDIENTS

1 5- or 6-ounce or 10.8 ounce package (5) refrigerated biscuits
All-purpose flour
1 tablespoon margarine or butter
2 tablespoons granulated sugar
½ teaspoon ground cinnamon
5 miniature milk chocolate kisses

1. Turn on the oven to 350°
Open the package of biscuits.
Separate the biscuits.

2. Sprinkle a small amount of flour onto a wooden board or pastry cloth. Place a biscuit on the floured surface. Use the rolling pin to roll the biscuit into a 4½-inch circle. Repeat with remaining biscuits. Place the biscuits on the ungreased baking sheet, leaving 2 inches between pieces.

3. Dip the small triangle-shape cutter into flour and use it to cut the biscuit with a

triangle point about ½ inch from the center of the circle. Repeat 5 more times to make the spokes of a wheel. Or, use the sharp knife to cut triangles from the dough to make the spokes of a wheel. Remove the cutouts. Place the triangle cutouts on the baking sheet.

4. Put the margarine or butter in the microwave-safe bowl. Cover with waxed paper. Microwave on high for 20 to 30 seconds or until margarine or butter is melted. (Or, put margarine or butter in the small saucepan. Put the saucepan on a burner. Turn burner to low heat. Cook until margarine or butter is melted. Turn off burner. Remove saucepan from burner.) Save until Step 6.

5. Put the sugar and cinnamon in the small bowl or custard cup. Stir with the spoon to mix.

6. Use the pastry brush to brush the edge of each wheel with the melted margarine or butter. Sprinkle the edge with the sugar-cinnamon mixture. Brush the triangles with the melted margarine or butter. Sprinkle with the sugar-cinnamon mixture.

7. Put the baking sheet in oven. Bake for 10 to 15 minutes or until biscuits are light brown. Turn off oven. Use the hot pads to remove the baking sheet from the oven.

8. Use the pancake turner to transfer the biscuit wheels and triangles from the baking sheet to the cooling rack. Press a chocolate kiss into the center of each wheel. Serve warm.

Nutrition Facts per snack: 142 calories, 5 g total fat (1 g saturated fat), 0 mg cholesterol, 296 mg sodium, 23 g carbohydrate, 0 g fiber, 2 g protein

LOG CABIN HOMESTEADS

Hankering for a homestead? Chicken salad holds these bread logs together.

INGREDIENTS

- ¼ cup chicken, tuna, or ham salad
- 3 slices whole wheat bread
- 1 slice American cheese
- 2 celery sticks, each cut 4½ inches long
- 2 carrot sticks, each cut 4½ inches long
- 1 chunk carrot, cut about 1-inch long

UTENSILS

- Measuring cup
- Table knife
- Small plate
- 4 wooden skewers

START TO FINISH: 15 MINUTES • MAKES 2 SNACKS

1. Use the table knife to spread the chicken, tuna, or ham salad over 1 slice of bread. Add the slice of cheese. Top with another slice of bread. Use the table knife to cut the sandwich lengthwise into 4 strips.

2. To build the cabin, place 1 sandwich strip on one side of the plate. Place another sandwich strip on the opposite side of the plate. Place the celery and carrot sticks on top of the sandwich strips as crosspieces. Top with the remaining 2 sandwich strips.

3. For the roof, fold the remaining slice of bread in half. Place on top of sandwich strips. For the chimney, place the carrot chunk onto the end of 1 of the skewers. Insert skewer with the carrot into 1 corner of the cabin.

4. Insert remaining 3 skewers into the other corners of the cabin for support.

Nutrition Facts per snack: 241 calories, 11 g total fat (3 g saturated fat), 22 mg cholesterol, 677 mg sodium, 27 g carbohydrate, 6 g fiber, 11 g protein

BLAZE-A-TRAIL MIX

Grab a handful and hit the trail on your next snacking adventure.

INGREDIENTS

2 cups honey graham cereal

1 cup tiny marshmallows

1 cup peanuts

½ cup semisweet chocolate pieces

½ cup raisins

UTENSILS

Measuring cups

Plastic bag or covered container

START TO FINISH: 10 MINUTES • MAKES 5 CUPS

1. Put the cereal, marshmallows, peanuts, chocolate pieces, and raisins in the plastic bag or covered container. Close the bag or container. Shake to mix.

2. Store the mix in the plastic bag or covered container in a cool, dry place for up to 2 weeks.

Nutrition Facts per ½ cup: 193 calories, 10 g total fat (1 g saturated fat), 0 mg cholesterol, 199 mg sodium, 25 g carbohydrate, 2 g fiber, 5 g protein

ABILENE

DODGE CITY

PONDEROSA

MAP

COOL DUDE DRINKS

Mosey on up to the counter for a mug of this fruity firewater.

START TO FINISH: 15 MINUTES • MAKES 10 (5-OUNCE) SERVINGS

1. Pour the cherry juice blend and lemonade concentrate into the pitcher; stir with the wooden spoon until mixed. Cover and chill until serving time.

2. Just before serving, carefully pour the sparkling water into the cherry juice mixture.

3. Fill glasses with crushed ice. Pour the cherry juice mixture into the glasses.

Nutrition Facts per serving: 93 calories, 0 g total fat (0 g saturated fat), 0 mg cholesterol, 7 mg sodium, 24 g carbohydrate, 0 g fiber, 0 g protein

FRUIT RAWHIDES

Trap a few apples and turn them into sweet, chewy strips that'll whip the worst stomach growls.

INGREDIENTS

- 1 6-ounce package dried apples
- 1¼ cups water
- ¼ cup granulated sugar
- Nonstick spray coating

UTENSILS

Measuring cups

Medium saucepan with lid

Colander

Electric food processor or blender

Rubber scraper

15×10×1-inch baking pan

Foil

Clear plastic wrap

Sharp knife

PREP: 20 MINUTES • BAKE: 30 MINUTES • STAND: 12 HOURS
MAKES 1 FRUIT ROLL (10 TO 12 SERVINGS)

1. Put the dried apples, water, and sugar in the saucepan. Put the saucepan on a burner. Turn the burner to high heat. Cook until mixture is boiling. Turn the burner to low heat. Cover the saucepan with the lid and simmer about 15 minutes or until the apples are very tender. Turn off the burner.

2. Place the colander in the sink. Carefully pour the fruit mixture into the colander and let the liquid drain into the sink.

3. Put the drained fruit into the food processor bowl or blender container and cover with the lid. Process or blend on high speed until mixture is smooth. Every now and then, stop the food processor or blender and scrape down sides with the rubber scraper, pushing the mixture into the blades.

4. Turn on the oven to 300°. Cover the baking pan with foil. Spray the foil with the nonstick coating. Pour the fruit mixture onto the baking pan. Use the rubber scraper to spread the fruit into a thin, even layer over the entire pan.

5. Put the baking pan in oven. Bake for 30 minutes; do not open the oven door. Turn off oven. Let fruit rawhide dry overnight in the oven.

6. The next day, remove the baking pan from the oven. Lift foil and fruit rawhide off of the pan. Peel fruit rawhide from foil. Roll up fruit rawhide. To store the fruit roll, wrap it in plastic wrap. Store in the refrigerator for up to 3 months. To serve, use the sharp knife to cut the roll into 10 to 12 slices.

Nutrition Facts per serving: 61 calories, 0 g total fat, 0 mg cholesterol, 16 mg sodium, 16 g carbohydrate, 2 g fiber, 0 g protein

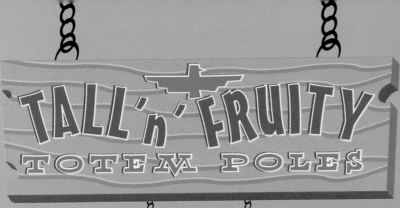

TALL 'n' FRUITY TOTEM POLES

Stack funny-faced marshmallows and fruit on a stick for a tummy-filling snack.

UTENSILS

- Small bowls or custard cups
- Clean, small paintbrushes
- Pastry brush
- 6- or 12-inch wooden skewers

INGREDIENTS

- 3 or 4 large marshmallows
- Food coloring
- ¼ cup cut-up fresh fruit such as apple, nectarine, kiwifruit, cantaloupe, honeydew melon, orange, pineapple, strawberries, and/or grapes
- Lemon juice
- Halved apple, if you like
- Caramel dip, if you like

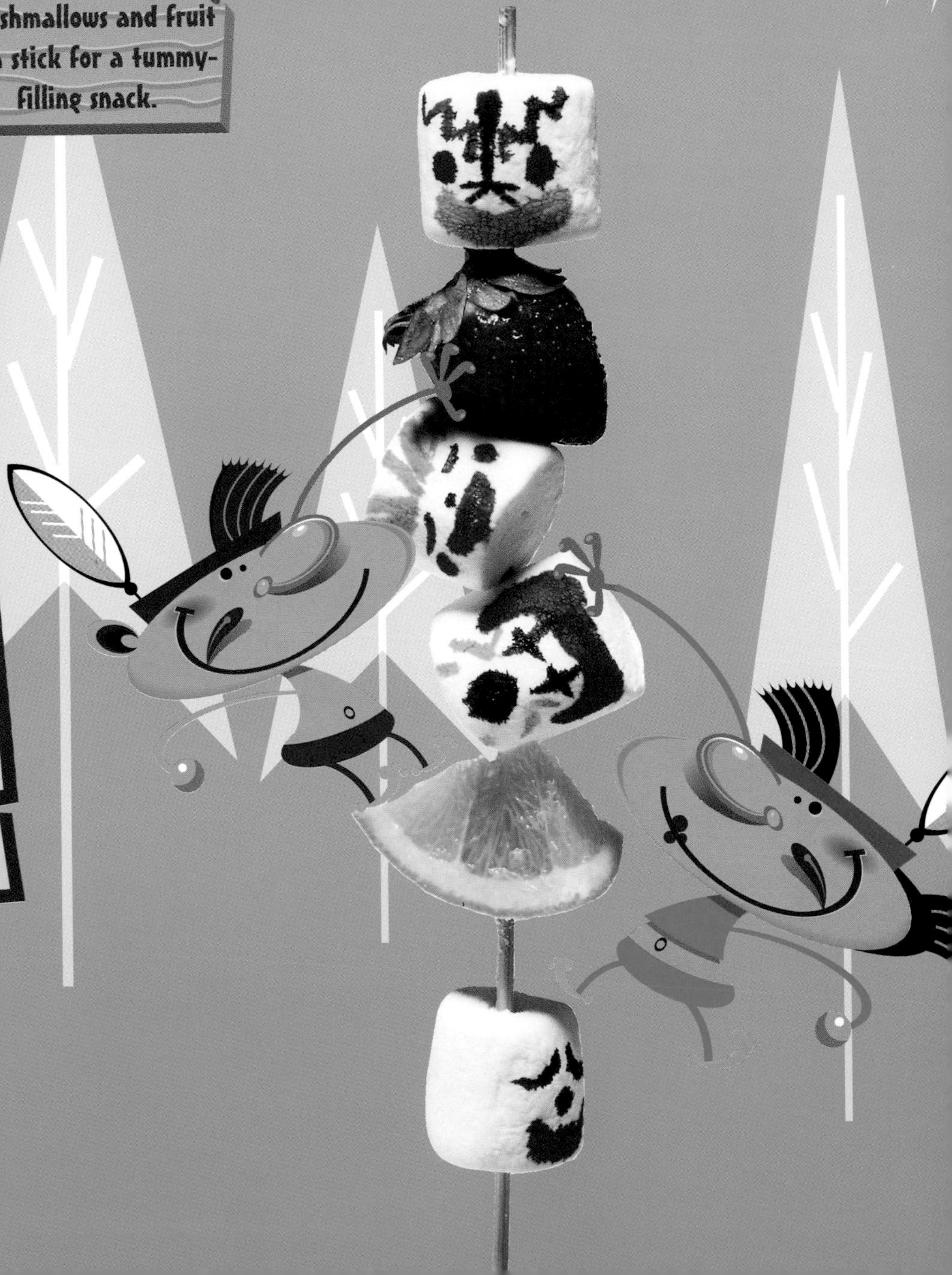

START TO FINISH: 15 MINUTES
MAKES 1 SNACK

1. For marshmallow faces, put a small amount of the food coloring into a small bowl or custard cup. (Use a different bowl for each color.) Use the food coloring and the paintbrushes to paint totem pole faces on the marshmallows. Let the food coloring dry.

2. If using apples or nectarines, use the pastry brush to brush the cut surfaces of the fruit with lemon juice to keep it from turning brown.

3. Push the skewer through pieces of fruit and the marshmallows.

4. If you like, to hold the totem pole upright, carefully stick the wooden skewer into an apple half.

5. To eat, remove fruit and marshmallows from skewers. If you like, dip into the fruit dip.

Nutrition Facts per snack: 60 calories, 0 g total fat, 0 mg cholesterol, 6 mg sodium, 15 g carbohydrate, 1 g fiber, 1 g protein

CARTLOAD O' NACHOS

Dig in and discover a gold rush of crispy corn chips loaded with all your favorite toppings.

INGREDIENTS

- 1 small tomato, if you like
- 4 cups baked tortilla chips (about 3 ounces)
- ½ of an 8-ounce package shredded Mexican cheese blend (1 cup)
- 2 to 4 tablespoons salsa
- Cooked bacon pieces, if you like
- Dairy sour cream or dairy sour cream dip (any flavor), if you like

UTENSILS

- Sharp knife (if using tomato)
- Cutting board (if using tomato)
- Large microwave-safe plate
- Measuring cups
- Measuring spoons
- Hot pads

MINE

START TO FINISH: 15 MINUTES • MAKES 4 SERVINGS

1. If using a tomato, use the sharp knife to remove the stem. On the cutting board use the sharp knife to cut the tomato into small pieces. Save until Step 5.

2. On the microwave-safe plate, arrange the tortilla chips in a pile to look like a mountain.

3. Sprinkle the cheese over the mountain of chips. Drizzle salsa over the chips.

4. Put the plate in the microwave oven. Microwave on high for 1 to 1½ minutes or until cheese is just melted, giving plate a half-turn halfway through cooking.

5. Use the hot pads to remove the plate from the microwave. If you like, sprinkle with the chopped tomato and/or cooked bacon pieces and top with sour cream or sour cream dip.

Nutrition Facts per serving: 279 calories, 10 g total fat (6 g saturated fat), 28 mg cholesterol, 298 mg sodium, 19 g carbohydrate, 2 g fiber, 9 g protein

Hare RAISERS

Watch these bewitching bunnies grow before your very eyes.

Utensils

Baking sheet

Foil

Waxed paper or paper towel

Large mixing bowl

Wooden spoon

Measuring spoons

Small mixing bowl

Spoon

Small microwave-safe bowl or small saucepan

Hot pads

Ruler

Clean kitchen towel

Pastry brush

Pancake turner

Wire cooling rack

Ingredients

Shortening

1 16-ounce package hot roll mix

2 tablespoons granulated sugar

1 teaspoon all-purpose flour

¼ teaspoon finely shredded orange peel

¼ teaspoon ground cinnamon

¼ cup margarine or butter

10 large marshmallows

Tubes of decorator icing

1. Cover the baking sheet with foil. Put some shortening on a small piece of waxed paper or paper towel and rub evenly over the foil to grease it. Save until Step 5.

2. Using the large mixing bowl and the wooden spoon prepare the roll mix as directed on the package, up to the point of shaping the rolls.

3. Put the granulated sugar, 1 teaspoon flour, the orange peel, and cinnamon in the small mixing bowl. Stir with a spoon until well mixed. Save until Step 5.

4. Put the margarine or butter in the microwave-safe bowl. Microwave on high about 30 seconds or until melted. Use hot pads to remove bowl from microwave. (Or, put the margarine or butter in the saucepan. Put the saucepan on a burner. Turn burner to low heat. Cook just until margarine or butter is melted. Turn the burner off. Remove saucepan from the burner).

5. For each rabbit, you will need 3 balls of dough. Make 1 ball 2 inches in diameter and 2 balls 1 inch in diameter. For the head, use your hands to flatten the large ball into a 3-inch circle. Dip a marshmallow into the melted margarine. Next roll the marshmallow in the sugar mixture. Place the coated marshmallow on the flattened dough circle. Wrap the dough around the marshmallow, pulling edges under to make a smooth top. Firmly pinch the dough together with your fingers to seal. Place the ball, seam side down, on the prepared baking sheet.

6. For the ears, roll each small ball between your hands into a 4-inch-long rope. Place the ears at the top of the head. Firmly pinch the dough together where the ears join the head to seal. If you like, fold an ear over so it looks floppy. Repeat with the remaining dough to make a total of 10 rabbits. Cover the rabbits with the clean kitchen towel. Let rise in a warm place about 30 minutes or until doubled.

7. Turn on the oven to 375°. Carefully remove the towel from the rabbits. Use the pastry brush to brush any remaining melted margarine over the rabbits. Put the baking sheet in the oven. Bake for 12 to 15 minutes or until golden. Turn off the oven. Use hot pads to remove baking sheet from the oven.

8. Use the pancake turner to transfer the rabbits to the cooling rack. Cool completely on rack. When rabbits are cool, use the tubes of decorator icing to pipe on faces.

Nutrition Facts per roll: 243 calories, 6 g total fat (1 g saturated fat), 21 mg cholesterol, 326 mg sodium, 41 g carbohydrate, 0 g fiber, 7 g protein

Abracadabra

Magic WANDS

With a wave of this coated pretzel, you can cast a spell over snack time.

Ingredients

½ cup vanilla milk pieces or 3 ounces vanilla-flavored candy coating, chopped

1 teaspoon shortening

10 long pretzel logs

Decorative candies or colored sugars

Utensils

Measuring cups

Measuring spoons

Small microwave-safe bowl or small saucepan

Wooden spoon

Waxed paper

1. Place the vanilla milk pieces or candy coating and shortening in a small microwave-safe bowl. Microwave on high for 1 to 2 minutes or until the mixture is softened enough to stir smooth. The mixture won't seem melted until stirred. (Or, put the vanilla milk pieces or candy coating and shortening in the saucepan. Place the saucepan on a burner. Turn the burner to low heat. Heat the pieces or coating until smooth, stirring all the time with the wooden spoon. Turn the burner off.)

2. Hold a pretzel over the melted mixture. Carefully spoon melted mixture over the end of the pretzel log. Place the wand on a sheet of waxed paper. Sprinkle the melted mixture with decorative candies or sugars. Repeat with remaining logs and melted mixture. Let stand at room temperature until the melted mixture becomes firm (about an hour).

Nutrition Facts per wand: 100 calories, 4 g total fat (2 g saturated fat), 3 mg cholesterol, 140 mg sodium, 15 g carbohydrate, 0 g fiber, 2 g protein

Abracadabra

29

Wacky Wizard Hats

Utensils
Baking sheet
Waxed paper
Measuring cups
Small mixing bowl
Wooden spoon
Spoon

Only whiz kids can make one disappear before it melts.

Ingredients
¾ cup ice cream (any flavor)

4 plain pointed ice-cream cones

4 chocolate-striped shortbread cookies

¼ cup chocolate-fudge ice-cream coating

Decorative candies

30

Prep: 30 minutes
Freeze: 3 hours • Makes 4 hats

1. Cover the baking sheet with waxed paper. Save until Step 3.

2. Put the ice cream in the bowl. Using the wooden spoon, stir the ice cream until it is soft.

3. Divide the ice cream among the ice-cream cones. Use the back of the spoon to make the ice cream level with the cone edge. Place a cookie on each cone with the chocolate side against the ice cream. Gently push the cookie against the ice cream so it will stick. Stand cones, cookie sides down, on the prepared baking sheet.

4. Put the baking sheet in the freezer. Freeze the cones for at least 3 hours.

5. Remove ice-cream cones from the freezer. Drizzle each cone with about 1 tablespoon of the ice-cream coating. Decorate with the candies, working quickly, before the coating becomes firm. Repeat with remaining cones, ice-cream coating, and candies. Serve immediately.

Nutrition Facts per hat: 185 calories, 6 g total fat (2 g saturated fat), 11 mg cholesterol, 112 mg sodium, 32 g carbohydrate, 0 g fiber, 3 g protein

Abracadabra

Pick-a-Card Cookies

Stack the deck in your favor when you deal your friends one of these crispy cookies.

Ingredients

1 18- to 20-ounce roll refrigerated sugar cookie dough

Red food coloring

All-purpose flour

Tubes of decorator icing, if you like

Small candies, if you like

Utensils

Cutting board

Sharp knife

Small mixing bowl

Wooden spoon

Pastry cloth

Rolling pin

Ruler

Table knife

1 ¾-inch heart-shape cookie cutter

Pancake turner

2 cookie sheets

Hot pads

Wire cooling rack

Prep: 20 minutes • Bake: 7 minutes per batch • Makes 12 cookies

1. Turn on the oven to 350°. Remove wrapper from the cookie dough. Place the cookie dough on the cutting board. Use the sharp knife to cut off ¼ of the roll. Save the remaining dough until Step 3.

2. Place the small piece of dough in the mixing bowl. Add several drops of red food coloring, stirring it with the wooden spoon, to make the dough pink. If necessary, use your hands to mix the dough and distribute the color evenly.

3. Sprinkle a small amount of flour over the pastry cloth. Place the white dough on the floured cloth. Use the rolling pin to roll the white dough to a 9×10-inch rectangle.

4. Use the ruler and table knife to divide the dough into 12 rectangles.

5. Cut a heart from the center of each rectangle with the heart-shape cutter, dipping the cutter into flour before each use. Using the table knife, carefully lift the hearts from the rectangles. If you like, save the hearts and bake as directed, below, reducing bake time.

6. Using the pancake turner, carefully transfer the rectangles to ungreased cookie sheets, leaving 2 inches between cookies.

7. Sprinkle more flour on the pastry cloth. Roll the pink dough to about ¼-inch thickness. Dipping the heart-shape cookie cutter into the flour before each use, cut the dough into hearts. Place a pink heart in the heart cutout in each rectangle on the cookie sheets.

8. Put one cookie sheet in the oven. Bake for 7 to 8 minutes or until the cookie edges are light golden brown. Use hot pads to remove the cookie sheet from the oven.

9. Use the pancake turner to transfer cookies to the cooling rack. Bake the second sheet of cookies the same way. Turn off oven.

10. If you like, when cookies are cool, use the tubes of decorator icing to draw queen faces. Decorate with candies, using icing to make them stick to the cookies.

Nutrition Facts per cookie: 173 calories, 7 g total fat (2 g saturated fat), 7 mg cholesterol, 178 mg sodium, 25 g carbohydrate, 0 g fiber, 2 g protein

Abracadabra

MAGIC BREW

Concoct a thirst quencher with just three secret ingredients: yogurt, juice, and soda.

Ingredients
1 8-ounce carton vanilla yogurt
1 cup orange juice
4 cups orange soda

Utensils
Measuring cups
Electric blender
2 ice cube trays
Clear plastic wrap
Drinking glasses

Prep: 10 minutes • Freeze: 6 hours • Makes 12 (½-cup) servings

1. Put the vanilla yogurt, orange juice, and 2 cups of the orange soda in the blender container. Cover blender with lid. Blend on high speed until combined. Turn off blender.

2. Pour the mixture into the ice cubes trays. Cover the ice cube trays with plastic wrap. Put the ice cube trays in the freezer. Freeze for 6 hours or overnight.

3. Just before serving, remove the frozen cubes from 1 of the ice cube trays. Put the cubes in the blender container. Add 1 cup of the orange soda. Cover and blend on high speed until slushy. Turn off the blender. Pour into 6 glasses. Repeat with remaining frozen cubes and orange soda.

Nutrition Facts per serving: 67 calories, 0 g total fat, 1 mg cholesterol, 22 mg sodium, 15 g carbohydrate, 0 g fiber, 1 g protein

Abracadabra

CHEESY Crystal Ball

You WILL love this blend of cheeses on fruit slices or crackers.

Ingredients

1 8-ounce package cream cheese

½ of an 8-ounce package shredded taco cheese (1 cup)

2 tablespoons margarine or butter

1 tablespoon milk

2 tablespoons apple jelly or strawberry jelly

Assorted crackers

Apple or pear wedges

1. Put cream cheese, taco cheese, and margarine or butter in the mixing bowl. Let stand at room temperature for 30 minutes.

2. Add milk to the cheese mixture in the mixing bowl. Beat with the electric mixer on medium speed until combined, stopping the mixer occasionally and scraping the bowl with the rubber scraper. Stop the mixer.

3. Cover the bowl with plastic wrap. Place the bowl in the refrigerator and chill for 4 to 24 hours.

4. Use your hands to shape the cheese mixture into a ball. Place the ball on the serving plate.

5. Put the jelly in the microwave-safe bowl. Microwave, uncovered, on high about 20 seconds or until melted. Use hot pads to remove bowl from microwave. (Or, put the jelly in the saucepan. Place the saucepan on a burner. Turn the burner to low heat. Cook until jelly is melted, stirring now and then with the wooden spoon. Turn the burner off. Remove saucepan from the burner.)

6. Use the pastry brush to brush the melted jelly over the cheese ball. Let stand about 15 minutes before serving.

7. Serve cheese ball with crackers and apple or pear wedges.

Nutrition Facts per tablespoon: 55 calories, 5 g total fat (2 g saturated fat), 13 mg cholesterol, 57 mg sodium, 1 g carbohydrate, 0 g fiber, 2 g protein

Abracadabra

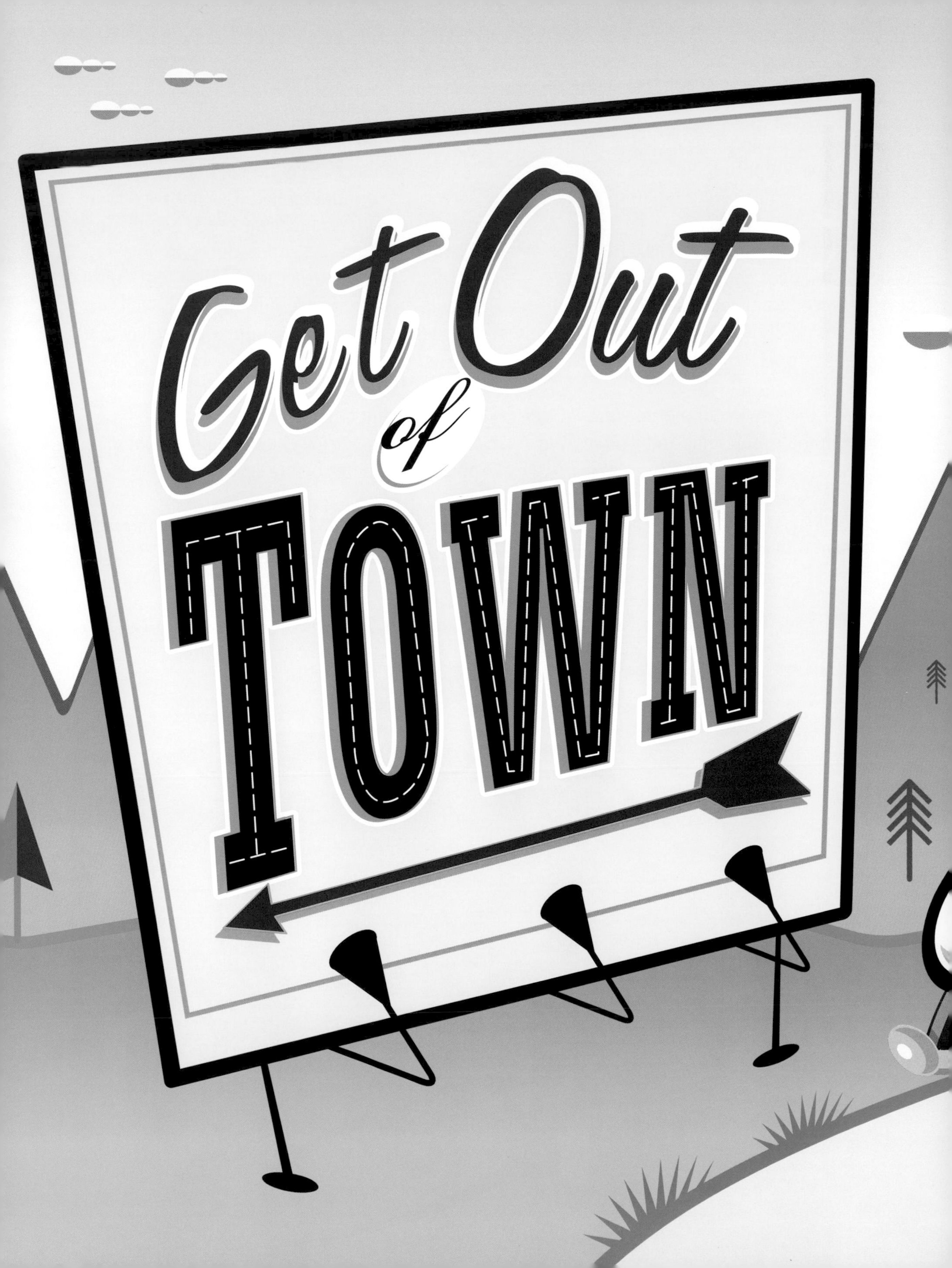
Get Out
of
TOWN

BUN BUGGIES

SLIP YOUR FAVORITE VEGGIE DIP INSIDE ONE OF THESE BUN BUGGIES AND DRIVE YOUR HUNGER AWAY.

Ingredients

- 1 hoagie bun
- 1 cucumber
- 1 small carrot
- 3 pitted ripe and/or pimiento-stuffed green olives
- ¼ cup dairy sour cream dip (any flavor)
- Vegetables cut into small pieces for dipping such as broccoli flowerets, sugar snap peas, zucchini, cucumber, and red, green, or yellow sweet pepper
- 1 pretzel, if you like

Utensils

Fork
Ruler
Cutting board
Sharp knife
Drinking straw
Toothpicks
Measuring cup

VEGGIE DIP

ONION DIP

1. Use the fork to scoop out the center of the top of the bun, leaving about ½ inch on the sides and 1 inch on the ends.

2. On the cutting board use the sharp knife to cut four ¼-inch-thick slices from the cucumber for the wheels. Use the knife to cut 2 thin carrot sticks, each about 4 inches long, for the axles. (Save any remaining cucumber and carrot and cut them up to use as vegetable dippers.)

3. About 1 or 2 inches from each end of the bun, push the drinking straw through the bun where the wheels will go to make holes for the axles. Next poke the straw through the centers of the cucumber slices. Throw away the straw. Slide the carrot sticks through the bun for axles. Attach the cucumber slices to the axles.

4. Stick a toothpick into 2 of the olives. Cut 2 slices from the remaining olive. Push a slice onto each toothpick behind the whole olive. Push the end of each toothpick into the front of the bun for headlights.

5. Fill the bun with the sour cream dip and vegetables. If you like, add a pretzel for a steering wheel.

Nutrition Facts per serving: 139 calories, 6 g total fat (0 g saturated fat), 0 mg cholesterol, 330 mg sodium, 19 g carbohydrate, 2 g fiber, 4 g protein

Get Out of TOWN

GET OUT OF TOWN
41

Stoplight Bites

Utensils

- Measuring cups
- Measuring spoons
- Medium mixing bowl
- Table knife
- Large mixing bowl
- Electric mixer
- Rubber scraper
- Wooden spoon
- Cookie sheets
- Ruler
- Wooden sticks, if you like
- Hot pads
- Pancake turner
- Wire cooling rack

Ingredients

- 1½ cups all-purpose flour
- ½ cup unsweetened cocoa powder
- ¼ teaspoon baking soda
- ¼ teaspoon baking powder
- ¼ teaspoon salt
- ½ cup butter
- 1 cup granulated sugar
- 1 egg
- 1½ teaspoons vanilla
- Red, yellow, and green candy-coated milk chocolate pieces or candy-coated peanut butter and chocolate pieces

1. Turn on oven to 350°. Put the flour, cocoa powder, baking soda, baking powder, and salt in the medium mixing bowl. Save until Step 4.

2. Use the table knife to cut up the butter. Put butter in the large mixing bowl. Beat with the electric mixer on medium speed 30 seconds or until butter is softened. Stop the mixer.

3. Add the sugar. Beat on medium speed until combined, stopping the mixer occasionally and scraping the bowl with the rubber scraper. Stop the mixer. Add egg and vanilla. Beat on medium speed until combined.

4. Add the flour mixture ½ cup at a time, beating as much of it in as you can with the mixer. Stop the mixer. Stir in as much of the flour mixture as you can with the wooden spoon. If necessary, use your hands to work the remaining flour mixture into the dough.

5. For each cookie, shape 1 tablespoon of dough into a 2½×1¼-inch rectangle on the ungreased baking sheet. Leave about 2 inches between cookies. If you like, push a wooden stick halfway into a short side of each rectangle.

6. Press red, yellow, and green candy-coated pieces into each rectangle for the lights on the stoplight.

7. Put the cookie sheet in oven. Bake for 8 to 10 minutes or until the cookie edges are firm. Use the hot pads to remove cookie sheet from oven. Let cookies remain on cookie sheet for 1 minute. Use the pancake turner to transfer cookies to the cooling rack. Repeat with remaining dough. If using just 1 cookie sheet, let it cool between batches. Turn off oven.

Nutrition Facts per cookie: 124 calories, 5 g total fat (2 g saturated fat), 18 mg cholesterol, 74 mg sodium, 18 g carbohydrate, 0 g fiber, 2 g protein

Middle of the Road Rascals

Ingredients

3 stalks celery

3 tablespoons apple-cinnamon or plain cream cheese in a tub or peanut butter

2 teaspoons honey

3 tablespoons chopped honey-roasted peanuts or chopped nut topping

About 12 animal crackers

Utensils

Cutting board
Sharp knife
Measuring spoons
Small mixing bowl
Rubber scraper
Table knife or small metal spatula

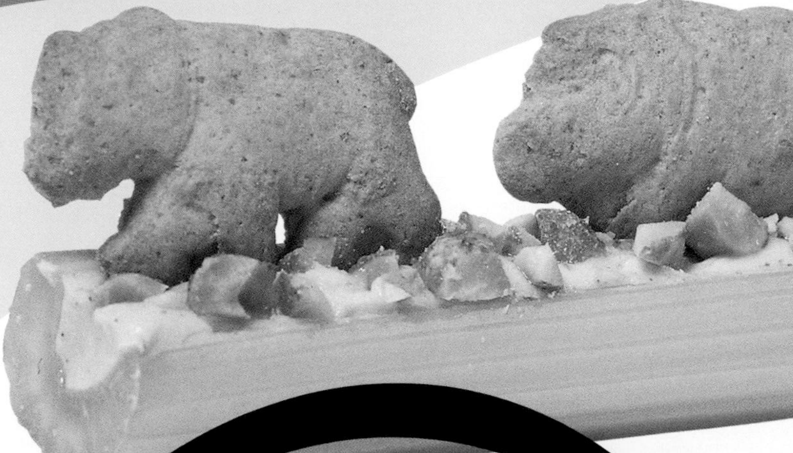

2. Put the cream cheese or peanut butter and honey in the bowl. Stir with the rubber scraper until mixed.

3. Use the table knife or small metal spatula to spread the cream cheese mixture in the celery sticks. Sprinkle chopped nuts on top of the cream cheese. Pat the nuts into the cream cheese with your fingers.

1. Place a stalk of celery on the cutting board. Use the sharp knife to cut off the white part at the base of stalk. Next cut off the leafy part at the top of the stalk. Throw away the trimmings. Repeat with the remaining celery stalks.

4. Place the filled celery stalks on the cutting board. Use the sharp knife to cut each stalk into 4 pieces. Push 1 or 2 animal crackers into the filling in each piece of celery.

Nutrition Facts per snack: 42 calories,
3 g total fat (1 g saturated fat),
5 mg cholesterol, 41 mg sodium, 4 g carbohydrate,
0 g fiber, 1 g protein

Get Out of TOWN

Smoothie Sailing

CRUISE THROUGH THE MUNCHIES WITH A FRUITY SMOOTHIE.

DRIVE-IN

Ingredients
- 1 medium banana
- 1 8-ounce can crushed pineapple (juice pack)
- 1 8-ounce carton vanilla yogurt
- 1 cup orange juice
- Orange wedges, if you like

Utensils
Cutting board
Table knife
Clear plastic wrap or small plastic bag
Can opener
Measuring cups
Electric blender
4 drinking glasses
Rubber scraper

PREP: 15 MINUTES (FREEZE BANANAS 2 HOURS AHEAD) • MAKES 4 (6-OUNCE) SERVINGS

1. Remove peel from banana. Place banana on cutting board. Use the table knife to cut the banana into chunks. Wrap banana chunks in plastic wrap or place in a small plastic bag. Freeze banana chunks for at least 2 hours.

2. Use can opener to open the can of pineapple. Put the undrained pineapple, frozen banana chunks, yogurt, and orange juice into the blender container.

3. Cover blender with the lid and blend on high speed about 1 minute or until mixture is smooth. Turn off blender. Pour drink into 4 glasses. Use the rubber scraper to get all of the drink out of the blender. If you like, place an orange wedge on the edge of each glass for decoration.

Nutrition Facts per serving: 144 calories, 1 g total fat (1 g saturated fat), 3 mg cholesterol, 34 mg sodium, 32 g carbohydrate, 1 g fiber, 3 g protein

Rocky Road-Test ICE CREAM

Ingredients

1 14-ounce can chocolate sweetened condensed milk
1½ cups milk or half-and-half
½ teaspoon vanilla
½ cup chopped nuts
½ cup tiny marshmallows
Crushed ice (about 8 cups)
Rock salt (about ½ cup)
Fudge ice-cream topping, if you like
Maraschino cherries, if you like

Utensils

Can opener
Measuring cups
1 clean small (12- or 13-ounce) coffee can with plastic lid
Measuring spoons
Wooden spoon
1 clean large (34.5- or 39-ounce) coffee can with plastic lid
Towel, if rolling cans on a surface other than cement
Dish towel
Rubber scraper
Ice-cream scoop

FALLING ROCKS

1. Use the can opener to open the can of sweetened condensed milk. Put half of the sweetened condensed milk (⅔ cup) in the small coffee can. Put the remaining milk in another container and store it in the refrigerator for another use. Add the milk or half-and-half and vanilla to the small coffee can. Stir the mixture with the wooden spoon until well mixed.

2. Add the nuts and marshmallows to the mixture in the small coffee can. Stir to mix. Put the lid tightly on the can.

3. Spread a thin layer of ice over the bottom of the large coffee can. Sprinkle 1 tablespoon rock salt over the ice. Put the small can inside the large can, lid side up. Pack the area around the small can with alternating layers of crushed ice and rock salt. For every 1 cup of ice you use, add 2 tablespoons salt. Put the lid tightly on the large can.

4. Roll the cans back and forth on a cement floor or sidewalk for 15 minutes. (Or, if you choose to roll the can on a countertop or other surface, cover the surface with the towel to protect it.)

5. Remove lid from large can. Lift out the smaller can. Wipe the side of the small can with the dish towel. Remove the lid.

6. Using the rubber scraper, scrape down sides and stir all the ice cream together. If the ice cream is too soft, repeat Steps 3 and 4. Roll the cans back and forth a few more minutes or until ice cream is firm.

7. Scoop the ice cream into serving bowls. If you like, top with fudge topping and cherries.

Nutrition Facts per serving: 377 calories, 28 g total fat (13 g saturated fat), 75 mg cholesterol, 91 mg sodium, 30 g carbohydrate, 0 g fiber, 5 g protein

QUICK·AND·EASY
Rocky Road Ice Cream
Place 1 pint of purchased chocolate ice cream in a large bowl. Stir the ice cream with a wooden spoon until soft. Add the nuts and marshmallows. Stir until mixed. If the ice cream is too soft, put it in the freezer until it becomes firm again.

Get Out of TOWN

Wafflescrapers

← →

UPTOWN, DOWNTOWN —IT'S AN URBAN JUNGLE OUT THERE.

Ingredients

- 2 frozen square or rectangular waffles
- 2 to 4 tablespoons jelly, peanut butter, and/or yogurt

Utensils

Toaster

Table knife

Waxed paper

Measuring spoon

1. Toast the waffles. Using the squares in the waffles as a guide, use the table knife to cut the waffles into different size pieces. Place the waffle pieces next to each other on a piece of waxed paper to create a city skyline.

2. Spread each skyscraper with jelly, peanut butter, or yogurt.

Nutrition Facts per waffle: 139 calories, 3 g total fat (0 g saturated fat), 0 mg cholesterol, 265 mg sodium, 27 g carbohydrate, 0 g fiber, 2 g protein

ON THE

Field-of-Greens PIZZA

If you plant the veggies on the pizza crust . . . they will come and eat!

UTENSILS

Baking sheet
Rolling pin
Ruler
Hot pads
Wire cooling rack
Measuring spoons
Small mixing bowl
Wooden spoon
Table knife or small metal spatula
Measuring cups
Clear plastic wrap, if refrigerating pizza
Sharp knife or kitchen scissors

INGREDIENTS

1 4-ounce package (4) refrigerated crescent rolls

½ of an 8-ounce tub (about ½ cup) fat-free cream cheese with garden vegetables

1 tablespoon milk

Dash garlic powder

Dash pepper

3 cups assorted fresh vegetables such as small broccoli flowerets; sliced carrots; cut-up red, yellow, and/or green sweet peppers; quartered zucchini slices; alfalfa sprouts

Prep: 15 minutes • Bake: 8 minutes • Makes 6 servings

1. Turn on the oven to 375°.

2. Open the package of crescent rolls and remove rolls. Carefully unroll the sheet of dough onto the ungreased baking sheet. Pinch together the perforations with your fingers. Use a rolling pin to roll the dough into an 8-inch square, or use your fingers to press the dough into an 8-inch square.

3. Put baking sheet in oven. Bake for 8 to 10 minutes or until lightly golden. Turn off oven. Use hot pads to remove the baking sheet from the oven. Place the baking sheet on the cooling rack. Let crust cool completely.

4. Put the cream cheese, milk, garlic powder, and pepper in the bowl. Stir with the wooden spoon until mixed.

5. Use the table knife or metal spatula to spread the cream cheese mixture over the cooled crust.

6. Arrange the vegetables in rows on top of the pizza to look like a garden. Serve right away, or cover with plastic wrap and put in the refrigerator for up to 4 hours. To serve, use the sharp knife or kitchen scissors to cut the pizza into six rectangles.

Nutrition Facts per serving: 106 calories, 4 g total fat (1 g saturated fat), 4 mg cholesterol, 303 mg sodium, 13 g carbohydrate, 1 g fiber, 6 g protein

Barnyard BUDDIES

Corral one of these critter cookies for an afternoon pick-me-up.

UTENSILS

Table knife
Measuring cups
Large mixing bowl
Electric mixer
Measuring spoons
Rubber scraper
Wooden spoon
Clear plastic wrap
Cookie sheets
Ruler
Hot pads
Pancake turner
Wire cooling rack

INGREDIENTS

¾ cup butter

⅔ cup shortening

1½ cups sugar

1 tablespoon baking powder

¼ teaspoon salt

2 eggs

1 teaspoon peppermint extract

4 cups all-purpose flour

Paste or liquid food coloring

Striped Pig

For the body, flatten a tinted ball of dough to about 2½ inches. Shape a very thin strip of untinted dough for the white strip down the middle of the body. Roll a small tinted ball for head. Use tinted and untinted doughs to make legs, tail, ears, eyes, and snout. Attach pieces by pressing them gently onto the body and head.

Fluffy Lamb

For the body, roll untinted dough into small balls of varying sizes; lay them on cookie sheet touching each other in a rough oval, leaving an opening for the head. Using tinted dough, add a small round ball for head and small ovals for the feet.

Prep: 1 hour • Chill: 2 hours • Bake: 18 minutes per batch • Makes 25 cookies

1. Cut up the butter with the table knife. Put butter and shortening in the mixing bowl. Beat with the electric mixer on medium speed about 30 seconds or until softened. Stop mixer. Add sugar, baking powder, and salt. Beat on medium speed until combined, stopping the mixer occasionally and scraping the bowl with the rubber scraper. Stop mixer.

2. Add eggs and peppermint extract. Beat on medium speed until combined. Beat in as much flour as you can with the mixer. Stop mixer. Stir in the remaining flour with the wooden spoon. Cover the bowl with plastic wrap and chill dough at least 2 hours or overnight.

3. Turn on oven to 300°. To color and shape dough, divide dough into portions, one for each color that you want to use. Use your hands to mix the food coloring into each portion, adding it slowly until the dough becomes the desired color.

4. Form dough into animal shapes about ½ inch thick on an ungreased cookie sheet, leaving about 1 inch between cookies. Work with the dough as you would clay to mold and assemble as suggested below.

5. Put the cookie sheet in oven. Bake for 18 to 20 minutes or until edges are firm and cookies look set but bottoms are not brown.

6. Use the hot pads to remove cookie sheet from oven. Use the pancake turner to transfer cookies to the cooling rack. Repeat with remaining dough. If using just 1 cookie sheet, let it cool between batches. Turn off oven.

Nutrition Facts per cookie: 217 calories, 12 g total fat (5 g saturated fat), 32 mg cholesterol, 126 mg sodium, 26 g carbohydrate, 0 g fiber, 2 g protein

Polka-Dot Cat

For the body, flatten a 2-inch ball of tinted dough. Attach a smaller dough ball of the same color for the head. For legs and tail, roll dough into 3 thin logs about 1¼ inches long. Use a mix of tinted and untinted dough for spots, ears, eyes, nose, and whiskers.

Merry Cow

For the body, flatten an oval of tinted dough horizontally to about 2½ inches across. Roll tinted dough into a log ½ inch wide and 2½ inches long. Cut into 3 equal pieces for legs and head. Roll untinted dough into small circles and flatten until thin for spots, udder, eyes, and nose. Roll tinted dough into a rope for the tail and into 2 small dots for the nostrils.

MOO juices

Milk these thick shakes for all they're worth.

INGREDIENTS

1 pint vanilla, chocolate, or strawberry frozen yogurt or ice cream

½ to ¾ cup milk

UTENSILS

Measuring cups

Electric blender

4 small drinking glasses

Rubber scraper

Start to finish: 5 minutes • Makes 4 (4-ounce) servings

1. Put the frozen yogurt or ice cream and milk in the blender container.

2. Cover blender with the lid. Blend on high speed until smooth. Turn off blender. Pour shakes into the glasses. Use the rubber scraper to get all of the drink out of the blender.

Nutrition Facts per serving: 168 calories, 6 g total fat (4 g saturated fat), 12 mg cholesterol, 73 mg sodium, 24 g carbohydrate, 0 g fiber, 5 g protein

Cookie Milk Shakes

Prepare milk shakes as directed above using either vanilla or chocolate yogurt or ice cream. Add 4 chocolate sandwich cookies or chocolate-covered graham crackers to the blended mixture. Cover and blend just until the cookies are coarsely chopped. Turn off blender.

Candy Milk Shakes

Prepare milk shakes as directed above using either vanilla or chocolate yogurt or ice cream. Add 6 bite-size chocolate-covered peanut butter cups or one 1⅛-ounce bar chocolate-covered English toffee, broken up, to the blended mixture. Cover and blend just until the candy is coarsely chopped. Turn off blender.

CHICKEN·FEED

When you're feeling a bit flighty, grab a handful of these sweet and crunchy nuggets—they're not for the birds!

UTENSILS

Measuring cups
Measuring spoons
Medium saucepan
Wooden spoon
13×9×2-inch baking pan
Hot pads
Foil
Plastic bag or covered container

INGREDIENTS

¼ cup apple jelly or your favorite flavor jelly

3 tablespoons granulated sugar

2 tablespoons margarine or butter

½ teaspoon ground cinnamon

1 cup rolled oats

½ cup peanuts or slivered almonds

¼ cup shelled sunflower seeds

¼ cup coconut

Prep: 12 minutes • Bake: 20 minutes • Makes 4 cups

1. Turn on the oven to 325°.

2. Put jelly, sugar, margarine or butter, and cinnamon in the saucepan. Put pan on a burner. Turn burner to low heat. Cook until the margarine or butter is melted and sugar is dissolved, stirring all of the time with the wooden spoon. Turn off burner. Remove pan from burner.

3. Add the oats, peanuts or almonds, sunflower seeds, and coconut to the mixture in the saucepan. Stir with the wooden spoon until mixed.

4. Pour the mixture into the ungreased baking pan. Spread the mixture in an even layer with the wooden spoon. Put the baking pan in the oven. Bake for 20 to 25 minutes or until lightly browned. Twice during baking, open the oven door and use hot pads to pull out the oven rack slightly; stir the mixture with the wooden spoon. Turn off the oven. Use hot pads to remove the pan from the oven.

5. Tear off a piece of foil that measures about 14×12 inches. Pour the mixture from the pan onto the foil. Cool completely.

6. To store, place the mixture in the plastic bag or container; seal or cover tightly. Store in a cool, dry place for up to 2 weeks.

Nutrition Facts per ½ cup: 198 calories, 11 g total fat (3 g saturated fat), 0 mg cholesterol, 131 mg sodium, 22 g carbohydrate, 2 g fiber, 5 g protein

HAYSTACK SNACKS

See if you can find the raisin "mice" hiding in the candy-coated chow mein noodles.

INGREDIENTS

- 1 3-ounce can (2 cups) chow mein noodles
- 1 cup cornflakes
- ½ cup raisins
- 1 12-ounce package (2 cups) peanut butter-flavored pieces

UTENSILS

Baking sheet

Waxed paper

Measuring cups

Large mixing bowl

Wooden spoon

Microwave-safe bowl or medium saucepan

Hot pads

2 spoons

Covered container

Start to finish: 15 minutes • Makes 15 snacks

1. Cover the baking sheet with waxed paper. Save until Step 5.

2. Put the chow mein noodles, cornflakes, and raisins in the large bowl. Stir with the wooden spoon until mixed. Save until Step 4.

3. Put the peanut butter-flavored pieces in the microwave-safe bowl. Microwave, uncovered, on high for 45 seconds. Use hot pads to remove the bowl from the microwave. Stir with the wooden spoon until smooth. If necessary, microwave for 15 to 45 seconds more, stirring after every 15 seconds. (Or, put the peanut butter pieces in the saucepan. Put the pan on a burner. Turn the burner to low heat. Cook until the pieces are melted, stirring all the time with the wooden spoon. Turn off the burner. Remove the pan from the heat.)

4. Pour the melted peanut butter mixture over the noodle mixture. Quickly stir the mixture with the wooden spoon until all of the mixture is coated.

5. Working quickly, use 2 spoons to drop the mixture onto the prepared baking sheet. Let stand at room temperature until firm. Transfer the haystacks to the container. Cover tightly and store in the refrigerator for up to 5 days.

Nutrition Facts per snack: 163 calories, 9 g total fat (3 g saturated fat), 0 mg cholesterol, 101 mg sodium, 19 g carbohydrate, 1 g fiber, 5 g protein

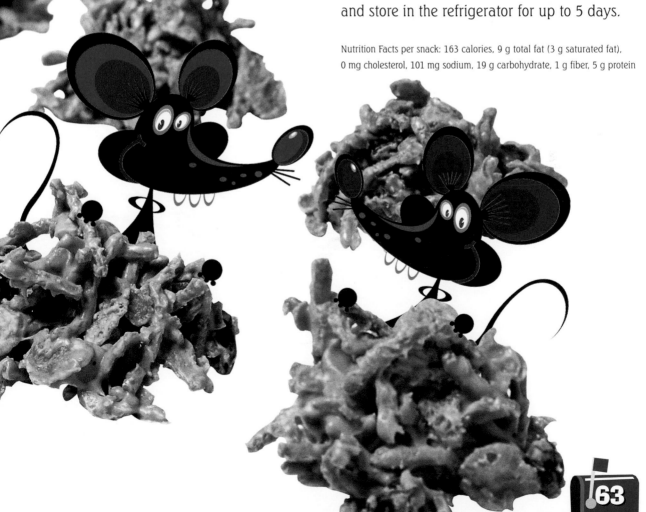

Sprouts, mushrooms, and tomatoes make these tortilla wraps anything but run of the mill.

SPIRAL SILOS

INGREDIENTS

1 7- to 8-inch flour tortilla

2 tablespoons dairy sour cream ranch or chive dip

2 slices very thinly sliced cooked beef, chicken, turkey, or ham (about 1 ounce)

¼ cup alfalfa sprouts or shredded lettuce

2 tablespoons finely chopped mushrooms

2 tablespoons finely chopped tomato

UTENSILS

Cutting board
Measuring spoons
Table knife
Measuring cup
Serving plate

Start to finish: 10 minutes • Makes 4 snacks

1. Place the tortilla on the cutting board. Spread the dip over the tortilla with the table knife.

2. Place the meat in a single layer on top of the tortilla. Top with alfalfa sprouts or lettuce, the mushrooms, and the tomato.

3. Roll the tortilla up tightly. Place the tortilla with the seam side down on the cutting board. Use the knife to cut off the uneven ends. Cut the remaining tortilla roll into 4 pieces. Stand the pieces upright on the serving plate so they look like silos.

Nutrition Facts per snack: 61 calories, 3 g total fat (0 g saturated fat), 8 mg cholesterol, 103 mg sodium, 5 g carbohydrate, 0 g fiber, 3 g protein

CORN COBS

Three kinds of corn—popped, puffed, and candy—give you three times the taste and crunch.

INGREDIENTS

3 tablespoons margarine or butter

4 cups tiny marshmallows

2 cups popped popcorn

2 cups puffed corn cereal

1 cup candy corn

Softened margarine or butter

UTENSILS

Waxed paper
Baking sheet
Measuring cups
Large saucepan
Wooden spoon
8 wooden sticks

Start to finish: 25 minutes • Makes 8 snacks

1. Cover the baking sheet with waxed paper. Save until Step 5.

2. Put the 3 tablespoons margarine or butter in saucepan. Put pan on a burner. Turn burner to low heat. Cook until margarine is melted.

3. Add the marshmallows to the saucepan. Cook until the marshmallows are melted, stirring all of the time with the wooden spoon. Turn off burner. Remove pan from the burner.

4. Add the popped popcorn and puffed corn cereal to the pan. Quickly stir the mixture with the wooden spoon until the popcorn and cereal are

coated with the marshmallow mixture. Stir in the candy corn. If mixture is too hot to touch, wait a few minutes until it cools slightly.

5. Rub some softened margarine or butter over your hands. Use your hands to shape the mixture into eight 4-inch-long logs, that look like ears of corn. Push a wooden stick into the end of each ear. Place on prepared baking sheet. Let cool completely. Serve the same day.

Nutrition Facts per snack: 253 calories, 6 g total fat (1 g saturated fat), 0 mg cholesterol, 157 mg sodium, 51 g carbohydrate, 0 g fiber, 2 g protein

SPACE

SPACE SHIP SALAD

5, 4, 3, 2, 1...
BLAST OFF! YOU'RE ON YOUR WAY TO AN EXPLOSION OF FRUIT FLAVORS.

INGREDIENTS

1 large banana

Lemon juice

2 slices canned pineapple

¾ cup low-fat cottage cheese

Melon slices, if you like

Blueberries, if you like

UTENSILS

Table knife

Pastry brush

4 salad plates

Spoon

Cutting board (if using melon stars)

1½-inch star-shape cookie cutter (if using melon stars)

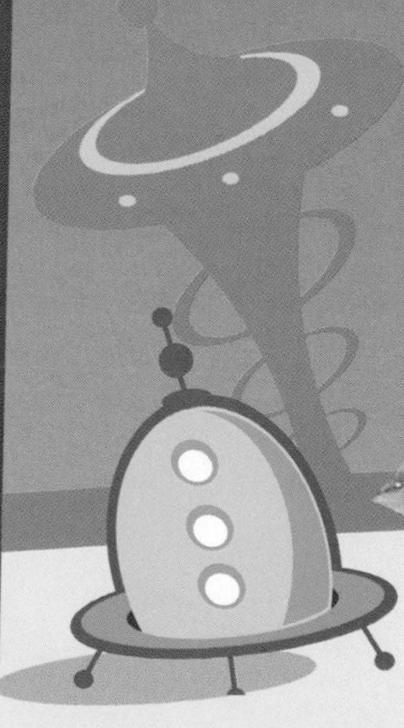

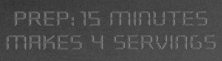

1. Remove the peel from the banana. Use the table knife to cut the banana in half crosswise. Then cut each half in half lengthwise. You will have 4 pieces. Use the pastry brush to brush banana pieces with lemon juice. Place 1 piece of banana in the center of each plate.

2. Use the table knife to cut each pineapple slice into quarters. Using 2 pieces of pineapple, place 1 on each side of a banana piece. Repeat with the remaining pineapple pieces and bananas. For smoke, spoon cottage cheese along the bottom of each banana.

3. If you like, for stars, place melon slices on the cutting board. Use the cookie cutter to cut stars from the melon. Arrange stars and blueberries on plates.

Nutrition Facts per serving: 90 calories, 1 g total fat (1 g saturated fat), 4 mg cholesterol, 173 mg sodium, 15 g carbohydrate, 1 g fiber, 6 g protein

Blast Off into OUTER SPACE

71

Shooting STARS

MAKE A WISH ON THESE TANGY, FRUITY STARS THAT MELT IN YOUR MOUTH.

INGREDIENTS

1½ cups lemon-lime carbonated beverage

3 envelopes unflavored gelatin

1 6-ounce can frozen orange juice or lemonade concentrate

Small decorative candies, if you like

UTENSILS

8×8×2-inch baking pan

Foil

Measuring cups

Medium saucepan

Wooden spoon

Clear plastic wrap

Cutting board

1½-inch star-shape or other shape cookie cutter or table knife

1. Line the baking pan with the foil so foil covers the bottom and sides of the pan. Press the foil into the pan where the sides and the bottom meet. Smooth out the foil with your fingers to remove wrinkles. Save until Step 3.

2. Pour the carbonated beverage into the saucepan. Sprinkle the gelatin over the beverage. Let stand for 1 minute. Put the pan on the burner. Turn the burner to high heat. Heat until mixture begins to boil, stirring all the time with the wooden spoon. Boil and stir until the gelatin dissolves. Turn off burner. Remove saucepan from burner.

3. Open the can of frozen juice concentrate. Stir the frozen juice concentrate into the hot gelatin mixture. Stir until the juice concentrate is melted. Pour mixture into the foil-lined pan. Cover pan with plastic wrap. Place pan in the refrigerator. Chill about 4 hours or until firm.

4. Turn the pan upside down on the cutting board to remove the gelatin mixture. Remove the foil from the gelatin. Use the cookie cutter or the table knife to cut the gelatin into shapes. If you like, sprinkle with candies.

Nutrition Facts per piece: 15 calories, 0 g total fat, 0 mg cholesterol, 2 mg sodium, 3 g carbohydrate, 0 g fiber, 1 g protein

Blast Off into **OUTER SPACE**

73

Beam Me Up BANANA MUFFINS

TRANSPORT YOUR TASTEBUDS TO A NEW DIMENSION WITH FRESH BANANAS, CHOCOLATE, AND CINNAMON.

INGREDIENTS

Shortening

1 tablespoon granulated sugar

¼ teaspoon ground cinnamon

1½ cups all-purpose flour

½ cup quick-cooking rolled oats

⅓ cup packed brown sugar

1½ teaspoons baking powder

½ teaspoon baking soda

½ teaspoon salt

½ teaspoon ground cinnamon

⅓ cup miniature semisweet chocolate pieces, crushed banana chips, or almond brickle pieces

2 ripe medium bananas

2 eggs

½ cup cooking oil

UTENSILS

Paper towel or waxed paper

Muffin-top pan with 9 cups or baking sheet

Measuring spoons

Small bowl

Wooden spoon

Measuring cups

Large mixing bowl

2 small mixing bowls

Potato masher

Fork

Rubber scraper

Hot pads

Wire cooling rack

Pancake turner, if needed

1. Turn on the oven to 400°. Put some of the shortening on a small piece of paper towel or waxed paper and rub evenly over the muffin-top cups or the baking sheet to grease. Save until Step 7.

2. Put the granulated sugar and the ¼ teaspoon cinnamon in the small bowl for the topping. Stir with the wooden spoon until mixed. Save until Step 7.

3. Put the flour, rolled oats, brown sugar, baking powder, baking soda, salt, and the ½ teaspoon cinnamon in the large mixing bowl. Add the chocolate pieces, banana chips, or almond brickle pieces. Stir with the wooden spoon until mixed. Save until Step 6.

4. Remove the peels from the bananas. Using the table knife, cut the banana into large pieces and put in a small mixing bowl. Use the potato masher or a fork to mash the bananas.

5. Crack eggs into the other small mixing bowl. Beat with the fork until yolks and whites are mixed together. Add oil and ¾ cup of the mashed bananas to eggs. Beat with the fork until ingredients are well mixed.

6. Add egg mixture to flour mixture. Stir with the wooden spoon until dry ingredients are wet. (The batter should be somewhat lumpy, not smooth.)

7. Spoon some of the batter into each prepared muffin-top cup. (Or, spoon batter, about ½ cup at a time, onto the prepared baking sheet, leaving about 3 inches between batter mounds.) Use the rubber scraper to remove all of the batter from the bowl. Sprinkle the sugar-cinnamon topping over batter.

8. Put muffin-top pan or baking sheet in the oven. Bake about 10 minutes or until muffins are golden. Turn off oven.

9. Use hot pads to remove muffin-top pan or baking sheet from oven. If using a muffin-top pan, carefully tip pan onto the cooling rack to remove muffins. If using baking sheet, transfer muffins to cooling rack with the pancake turner. Cool muffins on cooling rack about 10 minutes.

Nutrition Facts per muffin: 294 calories, 16 g total fat (2 g saturated fat), 47 mg cholesterol, 266 mg sodium, 36 g carbohydrate, 1 g fiber, 5 g protein

Blast Off into OUTER SPACE

Extra-Terrestrial PB&Js

EARTHLINGS CAN'T RESIST FACES THAT LOOK ALIEN BUT TASTE REMARKABLY LIKE PEANUT BUTTER AND JELLY SANDWICHES.

INGREDIENTS

2 slices bread

1 tablespoon peanut butter

1 tablespoon jelly (any flavor)

Raisins, if you like

UTENSILS

2 table knives

Measuring spoons

½-inch round cookie or hors d'oeuvre cutter, if you like

1. Cut the crusts from the bread slices with a table knife. Next, cut each bread slice into a shape that looks like the head of an alien. Eat the bread crusts and scraps or save them to make bread crumbs or croutons.

2. Spread peanut butter on a piece of bread with a table knife. Spread jelly on the peanut butter. Save until Step 5.

3. Use a clean table knife or a ½-inch round cookie or hors d'oeuvre cutter to cut 2 eyes in the remaining piece of bread.

4. Place the bread with the eyes on top of the jelly. If you like, place raisins in the eye holes.

Nutrition Facts per sandwich: 279 calories, 10 g total fat (2 g saturated fat), 0 mg cholesterol, 350 mg sodium, 41 g carbohydrate, 1 g fiber, 8 g protein

P. B. & B. Sandwich: Prepare sandwich as directed at left, except use banana slices in place of the jelly.

C. C. & J Sandwich: Prepare sandwich as directed at left, except use tub cream cheese in place of the peanut butter.

C. C. & R. Sandwich: Prepare sandwich as directed at left, except omit the peanut butter and jelly. Spread the bread with tub cream cheese. Sprinkle with raisins.

Blast Off into OUTER SPACE

CIRCLING SATELLITES

SEND YOUR HUNGER INTO ORBIT WITH FRUIT-STUDDED MEAT-AND-CHEESE-FILLED BISCUIT BITES.

INGREDIENTS

Shortening

½ cup shredded mozzarella cheese or pizza cheese (2 ounces)

¼ cup chopped fully cooked ham

2 tablespoons raisins, dried tart red cherries, or mixed dried fruit bits, if you like

1 4.5-ounce package (6) refrigerated biscuits

All-purpose flour

1 egg yolk

1 teaspoon water

Food coloring

UTENSILS

Paper towel or waxed paper

Baking sheet

Measuring cups

3 or 4 small bowls

Measuring spoons

Spoon

Wooden board or pastry cloth

Rolling pin

Ruler

2 or 3 forks

Pastry brush

Clean, small paintbrushes

Hot pads

Wire cooling rack

Pancake turner

1. Put some of the shortening on a small piece of paper towel or waxed paper and rub the shortening evenly onto the baking sheet to grease it. Save until Step 5.

2. Put the cheese and ham in a small bowl. If you like, add raisins, dried cherries, or fruit bits to the mixture in the bowl. Stir the ingredients together with the spoon. Save until Step 5.

3. Open the biscuit package. Separate the biscuits. Sprinkle a small amount of flour on a wooden board or a pastry cloth. Put 1 of the biscuits on the floured surface. Use the rolling pin to roll the biscuit into a 4-inch circle. Repeat with remaining biscuits.

4. Put the egg yolk and the water in a small bowl. Beat the egg yolk and water together with a fork until well mixed. Rinse fork. Use the pastry brush to brush some of the egg yolk mixture around the edge of each circle.

5. Place about ¼ cup of the ham mixture on each of 3 circles. Top with the 3 remaining circles, egg sides down, stretching the top circles to cover the bottom circles. Using the tines of the fork or your fingers, firmly press the edges of the biscuit circles together to seal. Place the rounds on the prepared baking sheet. Prick the tops of the rounds with the fork.

6. Turn on the oven to 400°.

7. Divide the remaining egg yolk mixture among 2 or 3 small bowls. Add 2 or 3 drops of food coloring to each bowl. Stir with clean forks until well mixed. Use the clean, small

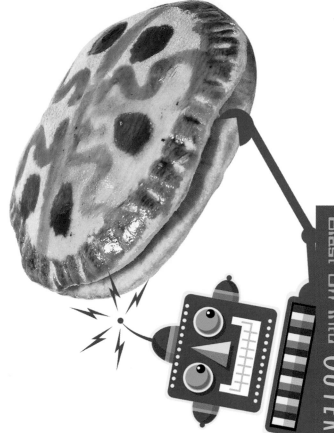

paintbrushes to paint designs on the rounds with the tinted egg yolk mixtures. If the tinted mixtures thicken while standing, stir in additional water, one drop at a time.

8. Put the baking sheet in oven. Bake for 10 to 12 minutes or until golden. Turn off oven. Use hot pads to remove baking sheet from oven. Transfer the rounds to the cooling rack using the pancake turner. Let stand about 5 minutes before serving to cool slightly.

Nutrition Facts per snack: 185 calories, 6 g total fat (1 g saturated fat), 84 mg cholesterol, 603 mg sodium, 23 g carbohydrate, 1 g fiber, 11 g protein

Blast Off into OUTER SPACE

Galactic GLACIERS

CHILL OUT OF
THIS WORLD WITH AN
ICY YOGURT POP.

UTENSILS

5 5-ounce paper cups

8×8×2-inch baking pan

Can opener

Colander

Measuring spoons

Electric blender or food processor

Rubber scraper

Foil

Table knife

5 wooden craft sticks

INGREDIENTS

1 15¼-ounce can pear halves or slices

1 8-ounce carton plain yogurt

3 tablespoons honey

½ teaspoon lemon juice

Few drops food coloring, if you like

Few drops almond extract, if you like

1. Put the paper cups in the baking pan. Save until Step 4.

2. Open the can of pears with the can opener. Place the colander in the sink. Empty the pears into the colander and let the liquid drain away.

3. Put the pears, yogurt, honey, lemon juice, and, if you like, food coloring and almond extract in the blender container or the food processor. Cover with the lid and blend or process on high speed until smooth. Turn off the blender.

4. Pour the mixture into the paper cups using the rubber scraper to remove all of the mixture from the blender container or food processor. Cover each cup with a square of foil. Use the table knife to make a small hole in center of each foil square. Slide a wooden stick through each hole and into the fruit mixture in the cup.

5. Put the pan in the freezer. Freeze for 4 to 6 hours or until the pops are firm.

6. To serve, remove the foil and tear the paper cups off the pops.

Nutrition Facts per pop: 111 calories, 1 g total fat (0 g saturated fat), 3 mg cholesterol, 36 mg sodium, 25 g carbohydrate, 2 g fiber, 3 g protein

Blast Off into OUTER SPACE

81

Over the Moon ROCKS

THESE COSMIC CLUSTERS WILL BRING YOU BACK TO EARTH WITH A CRUNCH.

UTENSILS

Measuring cups

13×9×2-inch baking pan

Microwave-safe bowl or medium saucepan

Waxed paper, if using microwave

Measuring spoon

Hot pads

Wooden spoon

Rubber scraper

Foil or large baking sheet

Very large bowl

Plastic bag or covered container

INGREDIENTS

3 cups puffed corn cereal

3 cups colored crisp rice cereal

3 tablespoons margarine or butter

¼ cup light-colored corn syrup

¼ teaspoon orange extract or cherry flavoring

1½ cups tiny marshmallows

1. Turn on oven to 325°. Place the puffed corn cereal and crisp rice cereal in the ungreased baking pan. Save until Step 4.

2. Put the margarine or butter in the microwave-safe bowl. Cover bowl with waxed paper. Microwave on high for 45 to 60 seconds or until melted. Using hot pads, remove bowl from microwave. (Or, put the margarine or butter in the saucepan. Put the saucepan on a burner. Turn burner to low heat. Cook until margarine or butter is melted. Turn off burner. Remove saucepan from burner.)

3. Add the corn syrup and orange extract or cherry flavoring to the melted margarine or butter. Stir with the wooden spoon until mixed.

4. Slowly pour the syrup mixture over the cereals in the baking pan. Scrape the bowl or pan with the rubber scraper to remove all of the syrup mixture. Use the wooden spoon to gently toss the cereal mixture until it is coated with the syrup mixture.

5. Put the baking pan in the oven. Bake for 7 minutes. Open the oven door and use hot pads to pull out the oven rack slightly; stir the mixture with the wooden spoon. Push the rack back in the oven and bake for 8 minutes more. Turn off the oven. Use hot pads to remove pan from oven.

6. Pour the cereal mixture onto a large sheet of foil or a large baking sheet. Spread the mixture over the foil or baking sheet to separate pieces. Cool for 15 minutes. Put the mixture in large bowl. Add the marshmallows; stir to mix with the wooden spoon. Store in the plastic bag or tightly covered container in a cool, dry place for up to 2 weeks.

Nutrition Facts per ½ cup: 82 calories, 2 g total fat (0 g saturated fat), 0 mg cholesterol, 128 mg sodium, 15 g carbohydrate, 0 g fiber, 1 g protein

Blast Off into OUTER SPACE

BODY BITS

Tiger teeth, lizard gizzards, and bat wings are just a few of the crunchy bits in this mischievous mix.

INGREDIENTS

2½ cups coarsely crushed blue corn chips

1 cup corn nuts

1 cup raisins

1 cup pretzel sticks

1 cup canned shoestring potatoes

1 cup cheese sticks

½ cup shelled pistachio nuts or peanuts

UTENSILS

Large serving bowl

Wooden spoon

Plastic bag or covered container

GIZZARDS

Bat Wings

START TO FINISH: 10 MINUTES•MAKES 8 CUPS

1. Put the crushed corn chips, corn nuts, raisins, pretzel sticks, shoestring potatoes, cheese sticks, and pistachio nuts or peanuts in the serving bowl. Stir to mix with the wooden spoon.

2. To store, place mix in the plastic bag or container; seal or cover tightly. Store in a cool, dry place for up 2 weeks.

Nutrition Facts per ½ cup: 157 calories, 6 g total fat (1 g saturated fat), 0 mg cholesterol, 215 mg sodium, 24 g carbohydrate, 1 g fiber, 3 g protein

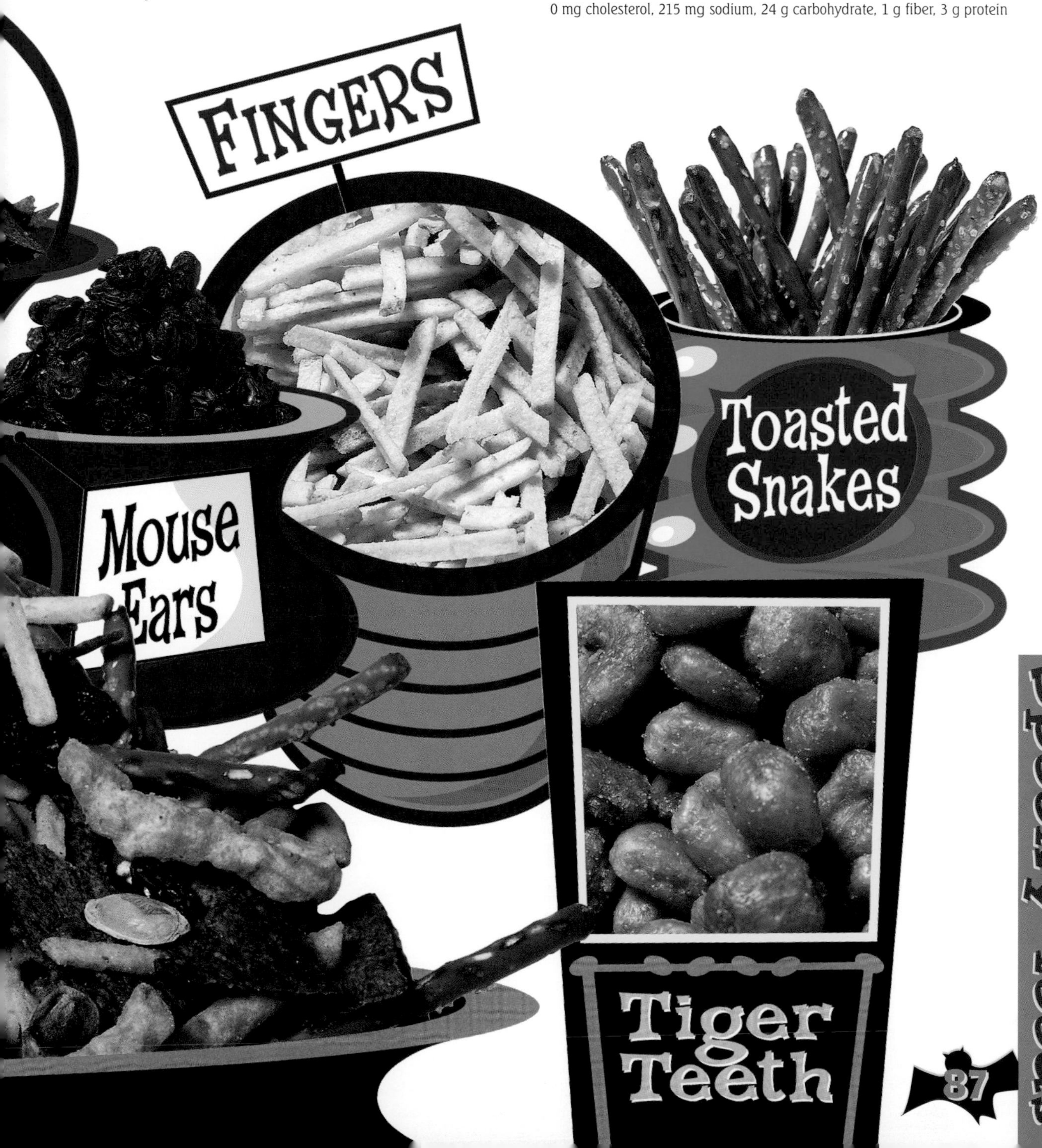
FINGERS
Toasted Snakes
Mouse Ears
Tiger Teeth

Slobber GOBS

Get your mouth around these ghoulish lips of apple with crunchy teeth.

INGREDIENTS
1 apple

2 tablespoons peanut butter or marshmallow creme

⅓ cup candy corn, broken pretzels, raisins, corn nuts, peanuts, and/or miniature semisweet chocolate pieces

UTENSILS
Cutting board

Apple slicer or sharp knife

Measuring cup

Measuring spoon

Table knife

Boo!

88

1. Place the apple on the cutting board. Use the apple slicer to cut the apple into slices. (Or, cut the apple into quarters with the sharp knife. Use the sharp knife to remove the core. Then cut each quarter into 2 slices.)

2. Use the table knife to spread 4 apple slices with peanut butter. Arrange the candy corn, pretzels, raisins, corn nuts, peanuts, and/or chocolate pieces on the peanut butter to look like teeth. Then top with another apple slice.

Nutrition Facts per snack: 98 calories, 4 g total fat (1 g saturated fat), 0 mg cholesterol, 58 mg sodium, 15 g carbohydrate, 1 g fiber, 2 g protein

Boo!

Boo!

Boo!

Spooky Foods

89

Witch's WARTS

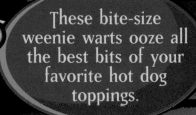

These bite-size weenie warts ooze all the best bits of your favorite hot dog toppings.

INGREDIENTS

1 jumbo turkey hot dog

Toppings such as chopped onion, chopped sweet green pepper, mustard, catsup, pickle relish, and finely shredded cheese

UTENSILS

Cutting board

Table knife

Ruler

Microwave-safe plate

Waxed paper

Hot pads

START TO FINISH: 10 MINUTES·MAKES 1 SERVING

1. Put the hot dog on the cutting board. Use the table knife to cut the hot dog into ½-inch-thick slices.

2. Place the hot dog slices on the microwave-safe plate. Sprinkle your favorite toppings over the slices.

3. Cover the plate with waxed paper. Microwave on high about 30 seconds or until warm. Use hot pads to remove the plate from the microwave.

Nutrition Facts per serving: 104 calories, 6 g total fat (2 g saturated fat), 30 mg cholesterol, 576 mg sodium, 6 g carbohydrate, 0 g fiber, 6 g protein

Creepy Kettles

Brew a stew of spiders and worms and you'll end up with cupcakes that squirm!

UTENSILS

- Waxed paper or paper towel
- Muffin pan with six 2½-inch cups
- Medium mixing bowl
- Wooden spoon
- Hot pads
- Wooden toothpick
- Table knife or small metal spatula
- Wire cooling rack
- Spoon
- Ruler
- Measuring cups

INGREDIENTS

- Shortening
- 1 8-ounce package brownie mix
- ¾ cup canned milk chocolate frosting
- ¾ cup prepared vanilla pudding or vanilla yogurt
- Chewy fruit worms, if you like
- Red string licorice, if you like

PREP: 20 MINUTES·BAKE: 18 MINUTES·MAKES 6 CUPCAKES

1. Turn on the oven to 350°. Put some of the shortening on a small piece of waxed paper or paper towel and rub evenly over the bottoms and sides of the muffin cups to grease them. Save until Step 3.

2. Prepare the brownie mix according to package directions using the medium mixing bowl and the wooden spoon.

3. Spoon some of the batter into each muffin cup, filling each half full.

4. Put the muffin pan in the oven. Bake for 18 to 20 minutes. (To test to see if the cupcakes are done, use hot pads to pull out the oven rack. Stick a wooden toothpick in the center of a cupcake; pull out the toothpick. If any cake sticks to it, push in oven rack, bake a few minutes more, and test again.) Turn off oven.

5. Use hot pads to remove muffin pan from oven. Place the pan on the cooling rack. Let the cupcakes cool in the pan for 5 minutes. Use the knife or a metal spatula to carefully loosen cupcakes from the muffin pan. To remove the cupcakes, gently tip the muffin pan over the cooling rack. Cool the cupcakes on the rack.

6. Turn the cooled cupcakes upside down. Using the spoon, carefully scoop out the centers of the cupcakes, leaving about ½ inch around the edges and about 1 inch on the bottoms of the cupcakes.

7. Spread the frosting on the sides and top of each cupcake with the knife or metal spatula. Spoon the pudding or yogurt into the centers of each cupcake. If you like, put some chewy fruit worms in the filling and/or push the ends of the licorice into opposite sides of the cupcake to make a handle.

Nutrition Facts per cupcake: 362 calories, 12 g total fat (4 g saturated fat), 38 mg cholesterol, 254 mg sodium, 59 g carbohydrate, 1 g fiber, 4 g protein

Spooky Foods

Bloody Good PHANTOM Faces

Add a frightful sight to an ordinary afternoon when you bring rice cakes to life with pudding and fruit.

INGREDIENTS

Assorted fresh fruits such as blueberries, raspberries, strawberries, bananas, kiwifruit, grapes, oranges, apples, pears, nectarines, peaches, plums, and/or star fruit (carambola)

2 4-ounce containers vanilla pudding

¼ cup dairy sour cream

1 teaspoon finely shredded lemon peel

4 plain rice cakes

2 to 3 tablespoons cherry or strawberry jelly

1. Use the sharp knife and the cutting board to cut up the fresh fruits. Save until Step 3.

2. Put the pudding, sour cream, and lemon peel in the mixing bowl. Stir with the spoon until mixed.

3. Use the table knife to spread about 2 tablespoons of the pudding mixture over each rice cake. Use the cut-up fruits to make a monster face on top of the pudding mixture.

4. Put the jelly in the microwave-safe bowl. Microwave on high for 20 to 30 seconds or until jelly is melted. Use hot pads to remove bowl from microwave. (Or, put the jelly in the saucepan. Put pan on a burner. Turn burner to low heat. Cook just until jelly is melted. Turn off the burner. Remove the pan from the burner.) Use the spoon to drizzle the jelly onto the fruit faces.

Nutrition Facts per snack: 170 calories, 5 g total fat (2 g saturated fat), 10 mg cholesterol, 97 mg sodium, 29 g carbohydrate, 0 g fiber, 3 g protein

Spooky Foods

Celebrate
the

easons

VALENTINE Parfaits

UTENSILS
Cutting board
Serrated knife
Ruler
Measuring cups
Sharp knife
Small mixing bowl
Rubber scraper
Spoon
2 parfait or sundae glasses

It's puppy love at first bite.

Start to finish: 15 minutes ✳ Makes 2 parfaits

1. Place the cake slices on the cutting board. Using the serrated knife, cut the cake into 1-inch cubes. Save until Step 4.

2. If using strawberries, place them on the cutting board. Use the sharp knife to remove the green stems. Slice the strawberries, cutting from top of each berry to the bottom. Save until Step 4.

3. Put the vanilla pudding and whipped cream or topping in the bowl. Use the rubber scraper to gently stir the whipped cream into the pudding. If you like, stir in red food coloring.

4. Place one-fourth of the cake cubes in the bottom of each glass. Add one-fourth of the berries to each glass. Top with one-fourth of the pudding mixture. Repeat the layers. Serve the parfaits immediately.

Nutrition Facts per parfait: 266 calories, 13 g total fat (7 g saturated fat), 45 mg cholesterol, 301 mg sodium, 34 g carbohydrate, 1 g fiber, 4 g protein

INGREDIENTS
- 2 1-inch-thick angel food cake slices
- ¾ cup fresh strawberries and/or raspberries
- 1 4-ounce container vanilla pudding
- ¼ cup whipped cream or thawed frozen whipped dessert topping
- 1 drop red food coloring, if you like

UNCLE SAM'S PIZZA

UTENSILS

Pizza pan or baking sheet

Measuring spoons

Spoon

Ruler

Cutting board

Sharp knife or kitchen scissors

1-inch star-shape cookie cutter

Hot pads

Wire cooling rack

Pancake turner

2 serving plates

Uncle Sam wants YOU to enjoy eating this stars-and-stripes pizza.

1. Turn on the oven to 425°. Put the Italian bread shell on the pizza pan or baking sheet.

2. Drizzle the pizza sauce over the bread shell. Use the back of the spoon to spread the pizza sauce over the bread shell to within ½ inch of the edge.

INGREDIENTS

1 4-ounce Italian bread shell (Boboli)

2 tablespoons pizza sauce

2 slices Canadian-style bacon or large pepperoni (1 to 2 ounces)

3 thin slices mozzarella cheese and/or cheddar cheese (1½ ounces)

Prep: *15 minutes* ✳ Bake: *5 minutes* ✳ Makes *2 servings*

3. Put the Canadian-style bacon or pepperoni slices on the cutting board. Cut the bacon or pepperoni into ¾-inch-wide strips with the sharp knife or scissors. Arrange the meat strips on the pizza to make 3 stripes.

4. Put the cheese slices on the cutting board. Use the star-shape cutter to cut the cheese. Place the cheese stars on the pizza, making a large circle around the edge of the pizza.

5. Put the pan in the oven. Bake for 5 to 7 minutes or until pizza is hot. Turn off the oven. Use the hot pads to remove the pizza pan from the oven. Place the pan on the cooling rack.

6. Cut the pizza into wedges with the sharp knife. Use the pancake turner to transfer the pizza to the serving plates. Serve immediately.

Nutrition Facts per serving: 254 calories, 9 g total fat (3 g saturated fat), 28 mg cholesterol, 851 mg sodium, 27 g carbohydrate, 1 g fiber, 18 g protein

GRAHAM CRACKER CABINS

INGREDIENTS

1 or 2 whole graham crackers

Canned vanilla, strawberry, lemon, chocolate, or cream cheese frosting

Assorted candies, nuts, almond brickle pieces and/or pretzels

UTENSILS

Waxed paper

Table knife

Summer cabins on a lake are sweet treats when built with crackers and candy.

Start to finish: 10 minutes ✳ *Makes 1 snack*

1. Cover your work surface with waxed paper. Put 1 graham cracker on the waxed paper. For a large cabin, use the whole graham cracker. For a small cabin, break the graham cracker into 2 squares and save 1 square for step 3.

2. For the cabin, use the table knife to spread frosting over the cracker on the waxed paper.

3. For the roof, break a whole graham cracker into 2 squares and set 1 aside for another use.

(Or, if making a small cabin, use the remaining cracker square from step 1.) Break the cracker square in half, making 2 rectangles. Spread each rectangle with frosting. Place rectangles at an angle on top of the frosted cabin overlapping at the top.

4. Press candies, nuts, brickle pieces, and/or pretzels into the frosting to decorate the cabin and the roof. If you like, for the large cabin use part of the remaining graham cracker square to make a door.

Nutrition Facts per snack: 310 calories, 3 g total fat (1 g saturated fat), 0 mg cholesterol, 100 mg sodium, 68 g carbohydrate, 0 g fiber, 1 g protein

MELTING snowflakes

Cheesy quesadillas will disappear just as quickly as the first snowflakes of the season.

INGREDIENTS

2 9- or 10-inch flour tortillas

½ cup shredded cheddar cheese (2 ounces)

Salsa, if you like

UTENSILS

Microwave-safe paper towel

Kitchen scissors

Microwave-safe plate

Measuring cup

Start to finish: 15 minutes ✳ *Makes 2 servings*

1. Place a tortilla on the microwave-safe paper towel. Microwave on high about 30 seconds or until soft. Cool slightly.

2. Fold the warm tortilla in half, then in half again. Use the kitchen scissors to cut out small pieces of the tortilla, just as you would to make a snowflake out of paper. Unfold the tortilla. Save until Step 4.

3. Place the remaining tortilla on the microwave-safe plate. Sprinkle with shredded cheddar cheese.

4. Place the snowflake tortilla on the cheese-topped tortilla. Microwave on high for 45 to 60 seconds or until the cheese is melted. Use the kitchen scissors to cut the quesadilla into 4 or 6 triangles. Serve with salsa, if you like.

Nutrition Facts per serving: 208 calories, 12 g total fat (7 g saturated fat), 30 mg cholesterol, 296 mg sodium, 15 g carbohydrate, 1 g fiber, 9 g protein

Gobblers

Gobble Gobble Gobble Gobble Gobble Gobble Gobble Gobble Gobble Gobble Gobble

Combine crackers, cheese spread, and a mix of yummy munchies for turkeys you can gobble.

INGREDIENTS

1½ teaspoons process cheese sauce or marshmallow creme

1 rich round cracker

1 bite-size rich round cheese cracker sandwich

5 to 10 crunchy cheese-flavored snacks, canned shoestring potatoes, and/or pretzel sticks

2 corn nuts or peanuts

1 small piece yellow sweet pepper or carrot

1 piece pimiento

2 raisins

Start to finish: 5 minutes ✳ *Makes 1 snack*

1. For the turkey body, spread cheese sauce or cream cheese on 1 side of the rich round cracker with the table knife.

2. For the head, press the cracker sandwich into the cheese sauce or cream cheese.

3. For the tail feathers, place the cheese-flavored snacks, shoestring potatoes, and/or the pretzel sticks about half of the way around the head.

4. For the feet, press the corn nuts or peanuts into the cheese sauce or cream cheese, extending the nuts slightly over the bottom edge of the cracker.

5. For the beak, place the piece of yellow sweet pepper or carrot on the cutting board. Use the sharp knife to cut a small triangular piece that looks like a beak. Next cut a small piece from the pimiento for the wattle. Use a little additional cheese sauce or cream cheese to attach the beak, the wattle, and the two raisin eyes to the head.

Nutrition Facts per snack: 105 calories, 6 g total fat (2 g saturated fat), 8 mg cholesterol, 325 mg sodium, 9 g carbohydrate, 0 g fiber, 3 g protein

Cheese and Cracker Gobbler Sandwich: Use 2 rich round crackers. Spread cheese sauce or cream cheese over 1 side of a cracker. Top with the other cracker. Continue with step 2, using cheese sauce or cream cheese to attach head. To fasten the tail feathers, push the ends of the cheese snacks, potatoes, or pretzels into the cheese sauce or cream cheese between the crackers. Continue with Steps 4 and 5.

Silly Season Cicles

Why wait for Christmas to enjoy one?

INGREDIENTS

- ¼ cup lime-flavored gelatin
- ¼ cup cherry-flavored gelatin
- 1 cup boiling water
- 1 6-ounce can frozen apple, orange, or pineapple juice concentrate
- 1 cup cold water

Prep: **25** *minutes*

Freeze: **5** *hours* ✳ Makes **8** *pops*

1. Place cone-shape plastic or paper cups inside the short drinking glasses for balance. Save until Step 3.

2. Put the lime gelatin in one bowl and the cherry gelatin in the other bowl. Add ½ cup of the boiling water to each bowl. Stir with the wooden spoon until the gelatin is dissolved. Add half of the can of the frozen fruit juice concentrate to each bowl. Stir until melted. Next stir ½ cup of the cold water into each bowl.

3. Use the measuring spoon to spoon about 1 tablespoon of the cherry gelatin into each plastic or paper cup. Cover each cup with a square of foil. Use the table knife to make a slit in the center of each foil piece. Push a wooden stick through each hole into the gelatin mixture. Put the pops, still in the drinking glasses, in the freezer. Freeze for 1 hour or until firm.

4. Remove the foil from the cups. Use the measuring spoon to spoon some of the lime gelatin over the frozen cherry gelatin in each cup. Put the pops, still in the drinking glasses, in the freezer. Freeze for 1 hour or until firm.

5. Repeat alternating layers of cherry and lime gelatin until the cups are full, freezing for 2 to 3 hours after adding the last layer or until firm.

6. To serve, hold a cup under warm water for a few seconds, being careful not to get water on the frozen gelatin. Pull the cup off the pop.

Nutrition Facts per pop: 76 calories, 0 g total fat, 0 mg cholesterol, 26 mg sodium, 19 g carbohydrate, 0 g fiber, 1 g protein

INDEX

Metric Cooking Hints

By making a few conversions, cooks in Australia, Canada, and the United Kingdom can use the recipes in **Better Homes and Gardens® Silly Snacks** with confidence. The charts on this page provide a guide for converting measurements from the U.S. customary system, which is used throughout this book, to the imperial and metric systems. There also is a conversion table for oven temperatures to accommodate the differences in oven calibrations.

Product Differences: Most of the ingredients called for in the recipes in this book are available in English-speaking countries. However, some are known by different names. Here are some common American ingredients and their possible counterparts:
- Sugar is granulated or castor sugar.
- Powdered sugar is icing sugar.
- All-purpose flour is plain household flour or white flour. When self-rising flour is used in place of all-purpose flour in a recipe that calls for leavening, omit the leavening agent (baking soda or baking powder) and salt.
- Light-colored corn syrup is golden syrup.
- Cornstarch is cornflour.
- Baking soda is bicarbonate of soda.
- Vanilla is vanilla essence.
- Green, red, or yellow sweet peppers are capsicums.

Volume and Weight: Americans traditionally use cup measures for liquid and solid ingredients. The chart, *top right,* shows the approximate imperial and metric equivalents. If you are accustomed to weighing solid ingredients, the following approximate equivalents will be helpful.
- 1 cup butter, castor sugar, or rice = 8 ounces = about 250 grams
- 1 cup flour = 4 ounces = about 125 grams
- 1 cup icing sugar = 5 ounces = about 150 grams

Spoon measures are used for smaller amounts of ingredients. Although the size of the tablespoon varies slightly in different countries, for practical purposes and for recipes in this book, a straight substitution is all that's necessary.

Measurements made using cups or spoons always should be level unless stated otherwise.

Equivalents: U.S. = Australia/U.K.

⅛ teaspoon = 0.5 ml
¼ teaspoon = 1 ml
½ teaspoon = 2 ml
1 teaspoon = 5 ml
1 tablespoon = 1 tablespoon
¼ cup = 2 tablespoons = 2 fluid ounces = 60 ml
⅓ cup = ¼ cup = 3 fluid ounces = 90 ml
½ cup = ⅓ cup = 4 fluid ounces = 120 ml
⅔ cup = ½ cup = 5 fluid ounces = 150 ml
¾ cup = ⅔ cup = 6 fluid ounces = 180 ml
1 cup = ¾ cup = 8 fluid ounces = 240 ml
1¼ cups = 1 cup
2 cups = 1 pint
1 quart = 1 liter
½ inch = 1.27 cm
1 inch = 2.54 cm

Baking Pan Sizes

American	Metric
8×1½-inch round baking pan	20×4-cm cake tin
9×1½-inch round baking pan	23×3.5-cm cake tin
11×7×1½-inch baking pan	28×18×4-cm baking tin
13×9×2-inch baking pan	30×20×3-cm baking tin
2-quart rectangular baking dish	30×20×3-cm baking tin
15×10×1-inch baking pan	30×25×2-cm baking tin (Swiss roll tin)
9-inch pie plate	22×4- or 23×4-cm pie plate
7- or 8-inch springform pan	18- or 20-cm springform or loose-bottom cake tin
9×5×3-inch loaf pan	23×13×7-cm or 2-pound narrow loaf tin or pâté tin
1½-quart casserole	1.5-liter casserole
2-quart casserole	2-liter casserole

Oven Temperature Equivalents

Fahrenheit Setting	Celsius Setting*	Gas Setting
300°F	150°C	Gas Mark 2 (slow)
325°F	160°C	Gas Mark 3 (moderately slow)
350°F	180°C	Gas Mark 4 (moderate)
375°F	190°C	Gas Mark 5 (moderately hot)
400°F	200°C	Gas Mark 6 (hot)
425°F	220°C	Gas Mark 7
450°F	230°C	Gas Mark 8 (very hot)
Broil		Grill

*Electric and gas ovens may be calibrated using Celsius. However, for an electric oven, increase the Celsius setting 10° to 20° when cooking above 160°C. For convection or forced-air ovens (gas or electric), lower the temperature setting 10°C when cooking at all heat levels.